# THIS BOOK BELONGS TO:

_____

_____

_____

_____

| Name: | ❖ Weather condition |
|---|---|
| Location: | |
| Date: | |

| ❖ Type of Forest | | ❖ surrounding plant | |
|---|---|---|---|
| ❑ Deciduous | ❑ Tropical | | |
| ❑ Coniferous | ❑ Other | | |

| **Stalk Characteristics** ❖ | Stalk shape | **Cap Characteristics** ❖ | Cap shape |
|---|---|---|---|
| | Stalk Color | | Cap Color |
| | Stalk Diameter | | Cap Diameter |
| | Stalk texture | | Cap Texture |
| | Stalk surface | | Cap Surface |
| | Stalk Length | | Cap Length |
| | Special Properties | | Special Properties |
| | | | Hymenium |

## Additional Notes

## *Species/Type*

| Name: | ❖ Weather condition |
|---|---|
| Location: | |
| Date: | |

## ❖ Type of Forest

| ☐ Deciduous | ☐ Tropical |
|---|---|
| ☐ Coniferous | ☐ Other |

## ❖ surrounding plant

| | |
|---|---|
| | |

**Stalk Characteristics**

| Stalk shape |
|---|
| Stalk Color |
| Stalk Diameter |
| Stalk texture |
| Stalk surface |
| Stalk Length |
| ❖ Special Properties |
| |

**Cap Characteristics**

| Cap shape |
|---|
| Cap Color |
| Cap Diameter |
| Cap Texture |
| Cap Surface |
| Cap Length |
| ❖ Special Properties |
| Hymenium |

## Additional Notes

| Species/Type |
|---|
| |
| |
| |

| Name: | ❖ Weather condition |
|---|---|
| Location: | |
| Date: | |

## ❖ Type of Forest

| ❏ Deciduous | ❏ Tropical |
|---|---|
| ❏ Coniferous | ❏ Other |

## ❖ surrounding plant

| | |
|---|---|
| | |

**Stalk Characteristics**

| Stalk shape |
|---|
| Stalk Color |
| Stalk Diameter |
| Stalk texture |
| Stalk surface |
| Stalk Length |
| ❖ Special Properties |
| |

**Cap Characteristics**

| Cap shape |
|---|
| Cap Color |
| Cap Diameter |
| Cap Texture |
| Cap Surface |
| Cap Length |
| ❖ Special Properties |
| Hymenium |

## Additional Notes

........................................................
........................................................
........................................................
........................................................
........................................................
........................................................
........................................................
........................................................
........................................................
........................................................

## Species/Type

| |
|---|
| |
| |

| Name: | ❖ Weather condition |
| --- | --- |
| Location: | |
| Date: | |

| ❖ Type of Forest | | ❖ surrounding plant | |
| --- | --- | --- | --- |
| ❑ Deciduous | ❑ Tropical | | |
| ❑ Coniferous | ❑ Other | | |

| Stalk Characteristics | | Cap Characteristics | |
| --- | --- | --- | --- |
| | Stalk shape | | Cap shape |
| | Stalk Color | | Cap Color |
| | Stalk Diameter | | Cap Diameter |
| | Stalk texture | | Cap Texture |
| | Stalk surface | | Cap Surface |
| | Stalk Length | | Cap Length |
| ❖ | Special Properties | ❖ | Special Properties |
| | | | Hymenium |

## Additional Notes

| Species/Type |
| --- |
| |
| |
| |

| Name: | ❖ Weather condition |
|---|---|
| Location: | |
| Date: | |

| ❖ Type of Forest | | ❖ surrounding plant | |
|---|---|---|---|
| ☐ Deciduous | ☐ Tropical | | |
| ☐ Coniferous | ☐ Other | | |

**Stalk Characteristics** ❖

| Stalk shape |
|---|
| Stalk Color |
| Stalk Diameter |
| Stalk texture |
| Stalk surface |
| Stalk Length |
| Special Properties |
| |

**Cap Characteristics** ❖

| Cap shape |
|---|
| Cap Color |
| Cap Diameter |
| Cap Texture |
| Cap Surface |
| Cap Length |
| Special Properties |
| Hymenium |

## Additional Notes

## Species/Type

| Name: | ❖ Weather condition |
|---|---|
| Location: | |
| Date: | |

## ❖ Type of Forest

| ❑ Deciduous | ❑ Tropical |
|---|---|
| ❑ Coniferous | ❑ Other |

## ❖ surrounding plant

| | |
|---|---|
| | |

**Stalk Characteristics**

| Stalk shape |
|---|
| Stalk Color |
| Stalk Diameter |
| Stalk texture |
| Stalk surface |
| Stalk Length |
| ❖ Special Properties |
| |

**Cap Characteristics**

| Cap shape |
|---|
| Cap Color |
| Cap Diameter |
| Cap Texture |
| Cap Surface |
| Cap Length |
| ❖ Special Properties |
| Hymenium |

## Additional Notes

........................................
........................................
........................................
........................................
........................................
........................................
........................................
........................................
........................................
........................................
........................................

| *Species/Type* |
|---|
| |
| |
| |

| Name: | ❖ Weather condition |
| Location: | |
| Date: | |

## ❖ Type of Forest

| ❏ Deciduous | ❏ Tropical |
| ❏ Coniferous | ❏ Other |

## ❖ surrounding plant

| | |
| | |

**Stalk Characteristics** ❖

| Stalk shape |
| Stalk Color |
| Stalk Diameter |
| Stalk texture |
| Stalk surface |
| Stalk Length |
| Special Properties |
| |

**Cap Characteristics** ❖

| Cap shape |
| Cap Color |
| Cap Diameter |
| Cap Texture |
| Cap Surface |
| Cap Length |
| Special Properties |
| Hymenium |

## Additional Notes

## Species/Type

| Name: | ❖ Weather condition |
|---|---|
| Location: | |
| Date: | |

## ❖ Type of Forest

| ❑ Deciduous | ❑ Tropical |
|---|---|
| ❑ Coniferous | ❑ Other |

## ❖ surrounding plant

| | |
|---|---|
| | |

| **Stalk Characteristics** ❖ | Stalk shape |
|---|---|
| | Stalk Color |
| | Stalk Diameter |
| | Stalk texture |
| | Stalk surface |
| | Stalk Length |
| | Special Properties |
| | |

| **Cap Characteristics** ❖ | Cap shape |
|---|---|
| | Cap Color |
| | Cap Diameter |
| | Cap Texture |
| | Cap Surface |
| | Cap Length |
| | Special Properties |
| | Hymenium |

## Additional Notes

## Species/Type

| Name: | ❖ Weather condition |
|---|---|
| Location: | |
| Date: | |

## ❖ Type of Forest

| ❑ Deciduous | ❑ Tropical |
|---|---|
| ❑ Coniferous | ❑ Other |

## ❖ surrounding plant

| | |
|---|---|
| | |

**Stalk Characteristics**

| Stalk shape |
|---|
| Stalk Color |
| Stalk Diameter |
| Stalk texture |
| Stalk surface |
| Stalk Length |
| ❖ Special Properties |
| |

**Cap Characteristics**

| Cap shape |
|---|
| Cap Color |
| Cap Diameter |
| Cap Texture |
| Cap Surface |
| Cap Length |
| ❖ Special Properties |
| Hymenium |

## Additional Notes

## *Species/Type*

| Name: | ❖ Weather condition |
|---|---|
| Location: | |
| Date: | |

## ❖ Type of Forest

| ☐ Deciduous | ☐ Tropical |
|---|---|
| ☐ Coniferous | ☐ Other |

## ❖ surrounding plant

| | |
|---|---|
| | |

### Stalk Characteristics ❖

| Stalk shape | |
|---|---|
| Stalk Color | |
| Stalk Diameter | |
| Stalk texture | |
| Stalk surface | |
| Stalk Length | |
| Special Properties | |
| | |

### Cap Characteristics ❖

| Cap shape | |
|---|---|
| Cap Color | |
| Cap Diameter | |
| Cap Texture | |
| Cap Surface | |
| Cap Length | |
| Special Properties | |
| Hymenium | |

## Additional Notes

## Species/Type

| Name: | ❖ Weather condition |
| Location: | |
| Date: | |

## ❖ Type of Forest

| ❑ Deciduous | ❑ Tropical |
| ❑ Coniferous | ❑ Other |

## ❖ surrounding plant

| | |
| | |

**Stalk Characteristics ❖**

| Stalk shape |
| Stalk Color |
| Stalk Diameter |
| Stalk texture |
| Stalk surface |
| Stalk Length |
| Special Properties |

**Cap Characteristics ❖**

| Cap shape |
| Cap Color |
| Cap Diameter |
| Cap Texture |
| Cap Surface |
| Cap Length |
| Special Properties |
| Hymenium |

## Additional Notes

## Species/Type

| Name: | ❖ Weather condition |
|---|---|
| Location: | |
| Date: | |

| ❖ Type of Forest | | ❖ surrounding plant | |
|---|---|---|---|
| ☐ Deciduous | ☐ Tropical | | |
| ☐ Coniferous | ☐ Other | | |

| *Stalk Characteristics* | | | *Cap Characteristics* | |
|---|---|---|---|---|
| | Stalk shape | | | Cap shape |
| | Stalk Color | | | Cap Color |
| | Stalk Diameter | | | Cap Diameter |
| | Stalk texture | | | Cap Texture |
| | Stalk surface | | | Cap Surface |
| | Stalk Length | | | Cap Length |
| ❖ | Special Properties | | ❖ | Special Properties |
| | | | | Hymenium |

## Additional Notes

.......................................................
.......................................................
.......................................................
.......................................................
.......................................................
.......................................................
.......................................................
.......................................................
.......................................................

| *Species/Type* |
|---|
| |
| |
| |

| Name: | ❖ Weather condition |
|---|---|
| Location: | |
| Date: | |

## ❖ Type of Forest

| ☐ Deciduous | ☐ Tropical |
|---|---|
| ☐ Coniferous | ☐ Other |

## ❖ surrounding plant

| | |
|---|---|
| | |

**Stalk Characteristics**

| Stalk shape |
|---|
| Stalk Color |
| Stalk Diameter |
| Stalk texture |
| Stalk surface |
| Stalk Length |
| ❖ Special Properties |
| |

**Cap Characteristics**

| Cap shape |
|---|
| Cap Color |
| Cap Diameter |
| Cap Texture |
| Cap Surface |
| Cap Length |
| ❖ Special Properties |
| Hymenium |

## Additional Notes

## Species/Type

| Name: | | ❖ Weather condition |
| --- | --- | --- |
| Location: | | |
| Date: | | |

## ❖ Type of Forest

| ❏ Deciduous | ❏ Tropical |
| --- | --- |
| ❏ Coniferous | ❏ Other |

## ❖ surrounding plant

| | |
| --- | --- |
| | |

**Stalk Characteristics**

| Stalk shape | |
| --- | --- |
| Stalk Color | |
| Stalk Diameter | |
| Stalk texture | |
| Stalk surface | |
| Stalk Length | |
| ❖ Special Properties | |

**Cap Characteristics**

| Cap shape | |
| --- | --- |
| Cap Color | |
| Cap Diameter | |
| Cap Texture | |
| Cap Surface | |
| Cap Length | |
| ❖ Special Properties | |
| Hymenium | |

## Additional Notes

## Species/Type

| |
| --- |
| |
| |

| Name: | ❖ Weather condition |
|---|---|
| Location: | |
| Date: | |

## ❖ Type of Forest

| ❑ Deciduous | ❑ Tropical |
|---|---|
| ❑ Coniferous | ❑ Other |

## ❖ surrounding plant

| | |
|---|---|
| | |

### Stalk Characteristics

| Stalk shape |
|---|
| Stalk Color |
| Stalk Diameter |
| Stalk texture |
| Stalk surface |
| Stalk Length |
| ❖ Special Properties |
| |

### Cap Characteristics

| Cap shape |
|---|
| Cap Color |
| Cap Diameter |
| Cap Texture |
| Cap Surface |
| Cap Length |
| ❖ Special Properties |
| Hymenium |

## Additional Notes

## Species/Type

| |
|---|
| |
| |

| Name: | ❖ Weather condition |
|---|---|
| Location: | |
| Date: | |

## ❖ Type of Forest

| ❏ Deciduous | ❏ Tropical |
|---|---|
| ❏ Coniferous | ❏ Other |

## ❖ surrounding plant

| | |
|---|---|
| | |

**Stalk Characteristics**

| Stalk shape |
|---|
| Stalk Color |
| Stalk Diameter |
| Stalk texture |
| Stalk surface |
| Stalk Length |
| ❖ Special Properties |
| |

**Cap Characteristics**

| Cap shape |
|---|
| Cap Color |
| Cap Diameter |
| Cap Texture |
| Cap Surface |
| Cap Length |
| ❖ Special Properties |
| Hymenium |

## Additional Notes

........................................................
........................................................
........................................................
........................................................
........................................................
........................................................
........................................................
........................................................
........................................................

| *Species/Type* |
|---|
| |
| |
| |

| Name: | ❖ Weather condition |
|---|---|
| Location: | |
| Date: | |

| ❖ Type of Forest | | ❖ surrounding plant | |
|---|---|---|---|
| ❑ Deciduous | ❑ Tropical | | |
| ❑ Coniferous | ❑ Other | | |

| Stalk Characteristics ❖ | | Cap Characteristics ❖ | |
|---|---|---|---|
| | Stalk shape | | Cap shape |
| | Stalk Color | | Cap Color |
| | Stalk Diameter | | Cap Diameter |
| | Stalk texture | | Cap Texture |
| | Stalk surface | | Cap Surface |
| | Stalk Length | | Cap Length |
| | Special Properties | | Special Properties |
| | | | Hymenium |

## Additional Notes

..............................................................
..............................................................
..............................................................
..............................................................
..............................................................
..............................................................
..............................................................
..............................................................
..............................................................
..............................................................
..............................................................

| *Species/Type* |
|---|
| |
| |
| |

| Name: | ❖ Weather condition |
|---|---|
| Location: | |
| Date: | |

## ❖ Type of Forest

| ☐ Deciduous | ☐ Tropical |
|---|---|
| ☐ Coniferous | ☐ Other |

## ❖ surrounding plant

| | |
|---|---|
| | |

**Stalk Characteristics**

| Stalk shape |
|---|
| Stalk Color |
| Stalk Diameter |
| Stalk texture |
| Stalk surface |
| Stalk Length |
| Special Properties |
| |

**Cap Characteristics**

| Cap shape |
|---|
| Cap Color |
| Cap Diameter |
| Cap Texture |
| Cap Surface |
| Cap Length |
| Special Properties |
| Hymenium |

## Additional Notes

.................................................
.................................................
.................................................
.................................................
.................................................
.................................................
.................................................
.................................................
.................................................
.................................................
.................................................

| *Species/Type* |
|---|
| |
| |
| |

| Name: | ❖ Weather condition |
|---|---|
| Location: | |
| Date: | |

## ❖ Type of Forest

| ❑ Deciduous | ❑ Tropical |
|---|---|
| ❑ Coniferous | ❑ Other |

## ❖ surrounding plant

| | |
|---|---|
| | |

**Stalk Characteristics** ❖

| Stalk shape |
|---|
| Stalk Color |
| Stalk Diameter |
| Stalk texture |
| Stalk surface |
| Stalk Length |
| Special Properties |
| |

**Cap Characteristics** ❖

| Cap shape |
|---|
| Cap Color |
| Cap Diameter |
| Cap Texture |
| Cap Surface |
| Cap Length |
| Special Properties |
| Hymenium |

## Additional Notes

### Species/Type

| |
|---|
| |
| |

| Name: | ❖ Weather condition |
|---|---|
| Location: | |
| Date: | |

## ❖ Type of Forest

| ❑ Deciduous | ❑ Tropical |
|---|---|
| ❑ Coniferous | ❑ Other |

## ❖ surrounding plant

| | |
|---|---|
| | |

**Stalk Characteristics**

| Stalk shape | |
|---|---|
| Stalk Color | |
| Stalk Diameter | |
| Stalk texture | |
| Stalk surface | |
| Stalk Length | |
| ❖ Special Properties | |
| | |

**Cap Characteristics**

| Cap shape | |
|---|---|
| Cap Color | |
| Cap Diameter | |
| Cap Texture | |
| Cap Surface | |
| Cap Length | |
| ❖ Special Properties | |
| Hymenium | |

## Additional Notes

........................................
........................................
........................................
........................................
........................................
........................................
........................................
........................................
........................................
........................................
........................................

## *Species/Type*

| |
|---|
| |
| |

| Name: | ❖ Weather condition |
|---|---|
| Location: | |
| Date: | |

## ❖ Type of Forest

| ❑ Deciduous | ❑ Tropical |
|---|---|
| ❑ Coniferous | ❑ Other |

## ❖ surrounding plant

| | |
|---|---|
| | |

**Stalk Characteristics**

| Stalk shape |
|---|
| Stalk Color |
| Stalk Diameter |
| Stalk texture |
| Stalk surface |
| Stalk Length |
| ❖ Special Properties |
| |

**Cap Characteristics**

| Cap shape |
|---|
| Cap Color |
| Cap Diameter |
| Cap Texture |
| Cap Surface |
| Cap Length |
| ❖ Special Properties |
| Hymenium |

## Additional Notes

## *Species/Type*

| |
|---|
| |
| |

| Name: | ❖ Weather condition |
|---|---|
| Location: | |
| Date: | |

| ❖ Type of Forest | | ❖ surrounding plant | |
|---|---|---|---|
| ❑ Deciduous | ❑ Tropical | | |
| ❑ Coniferous | ❑ Other | | |

**Stalk Characteristics** ❖

| Stalk shape |
|---|
| Stalk Color |
| Stalk Diameter |
| Stalk texture |
| Stalk surface |
| Stalk Length |
| Special Properties |
| |

**Cap Characteristics** ❖

| Cap shape |
|---|
| Cap Color |
| Cap Diameter |
| Cap Texture |
| Cap Surface |
| Cap Length |
| Special Properties |
| Hymenium |

## Additional Notes

...................................................
...................................................
...................................................
...................................................
...................................................
...................................................
...................................................
...................................................
...................................................
...................................................
...................................................

| *Species/Type* |
|---|
| |
| |
| |

| Name: | ❖ Weather condition |
|---|---|
| Location: | |
| Date: | |

## ❖ Type of Forest

| ☐ Deciduous | ☐ Tropical |
|---|---|
| ☐ Coniferous | ☐ Other |

## ❖ surrounding plant

| | |
|---|---|
| | |

**Stalk Characteristics** ❖

| Stalk shape |
|---|
| Stalk Color |
| Stalk Diameter |
| Stalk texture |
| Stalk surface |
| Stalk Length |
| Special Properties |
| |

**Cap Characteristics** ❖

| Cap shape |
|---|
| Cap Color |
| Cap Diameter |
| Cap Texture |
| Cap Surface |
| Cap Length |
| Special Properties |
| Hymenium |

## Additional Notes

## Species/Type

| Name: | ❖ Weather condition |
|---|---|
| Location: | |
| Date: | |

| ❖ Type of Forest | | ❖ surrounding plant | |
|---|---|---|---|
| ❏ Deciduous | ❏ Tropical | | |
| ❏ Coniferous | ❏ Other | | |

| **Stalk Characteristics** | | **Cap Characteristics** | |
|---|---|---|---|
| | Stalk shape | | Cap shape |
| | Stalk Color | | Cap Color |
| | Stalk Diameter | | Cap Diameter |
| | Stalk texture | | Cap Texture |
| | Stalk surface | | Cap Surface |
| | Stalk Length | | Cap Length |
| ❖ | Special Properties | ❖ | Special Properties |
| | | | Hymenium |

## Additional Notes

...........................................................
...........................................................
...........................................................
...........................................................
...........................................................
...........................................................
...........................................................
...........................................................
...........................................................
...........................................................
...........................................................
...........................................................
...........................................................
...........................................................

| *Species/Type* |
|---|
| |
| |
| |

| Name: | ❖ Weather condition |
|---|---|
| Location: | |
| Date: | |

## ❖ Type of Forest

| ❑ Deciduous | ❑ Tropical |
|---|---|
| ❑ Coniferous | ❑ Other |

## ❖ surrounding plant

| | |
|---|---|
| | |

### Stalk Characteristics

| Stalk shape |
|---|
| Stalk Color |
| Stalk Diameter |
| Stalk texture |
| Stalk surface |
| Stalk Length |
| ❖ Special Properties |
| |

### Cap Characteristics

| Cap shape |
|---|
| Cap Color |
| Cap Diameter |
| Cap Texture |
| Cap Surface |
| Cap Length |
| ❖ Special Properties |
| Hymenium |

## Additional Notes

## Species/Type

| Name: | ❖ Weather condition |
|---|---|
| Location: | |
| Date: | |

| ❖ Type of Forest | | ❖ surrounding plant | |
|---|---|---|---|
| ❑ Deciduous | ❑ Tropical | | |
| ❑ Coniferous | ❑ Other | | |

| **Stalk Characteristics** | | **Cap Characteristics** | |
|---|---|---|---|
| | Stalk shape | | Cap shape |
| | Stalk Color | | Cap Color |
| | Stalk Diameter | | Cap Diameter |
| | Stalk texture | | Cap Texture |
| | Stalk surface | | Cap Surface |
| | Stalk Length | | Cap Length |
| ❖ | Special Properties | ❖ | Special Properties |
| | | | Hymenium |

## Additional Notes

..........................................................
..........................................................
..........................................................
..........................................................
..........................................................
..........................................................
..........................................................
..........................................................
..........................................................
..........................................................
..........................................................
..........................................................

| *Species/Type* |
|---|
| |
| |
| |

| Name: | ❖ Weather condition |
| Location: | |
| Date: | |

| ❖ Type of Forest | | ❖ surrounding plant | |
|---|---|---|---|
| ❏ Deciduous | ❏ Tropical | | |
| ❏ Coniferous | ❏ Other | | |

| Stalk Characteristics ❖ | | Cap Characteristics ❖ | |
|---|---|---|---|
| | Stalk shape | | Cap shape |
| | Stalk Color | | Cap Color |
| | Stalk Diameter | | Cap Diameter |
| | Stalk texture | | Cap Texture |
| | Stalk surface | | Cap Surface |
| | Stalk Length | | Cap Length |
| | Special Properties | | Special Properties |
| | | | Hymenium |

## Additional Notes

| Species/Type |
|---|
| |
| |
| |

| Name: | ❖ Weather condition |
|---|---|
| Location: | |
| Date: | |

## ❖ Type of Forest

| ❑ Deciduous | ❑ Tropical |
|---|---|
| ❑ Coniferous | ❑ Other |

## ❖ surrounding plant

| | |
|---|---|
| | |

## Stalk Characteristics

| Stalk shape | |
|---|---|
| Stalk Color | |
| Stalk Diameter | |
| Stalk texture | |
| Stalk surface | |
| Stalk Length | |
| ❖ Special Properties | |

## Cap Characteristics

| Cap shape | |
|---|---|
| Cap Color | |
| Cap Diameter | |
| Cap Texture | |
| Cap Surface | |
| Cap Length | |
| ❖ Special Properties | |
| Hymenium | |

## Additional Notes

## Species/Type

| Name: | ❖ Weather condition |
|---|---|
| Location: | |
| Date: | |

## ❖ Type of Forest

| ❖ surrounding plant | |
|---|---|
| | |
| | |

| Type of Forest | |
|---|---|
| ☐ Deciduous | ☐ Tropical |
| ☐ Coniferous | ☐ Other |

### Stalk Characteristics

| Stalk shape |
|---|
| Stalk Color |
| Stalk Diameter |
| Stalk texture |
| Stalk surface |
| Stalk Length |
| ❖ Special Properties |
| |

### Cap Characteristics

| Cap shape |
|---|
| Cap Color |
| Cap Diameter |
| Cap Texture |
| Cap Surface |
| Cap Length |
| ❖ Special Properties |
| Hymenium |

## Additional Notes

## Species/Type

| Name: | ❖ Weather condition |
|---|---|
| Location: | |
| Date: | |

| ❖ Type of Forest | | ❖ surrounding plant | |
|---|---|---|---|
| ❑ Deciduous | ❑ Tropical | | |
| ❑ Coniferous | ❑ Other | | |

**Stalk Characteristics ❖**

| Stalk shape |
|---|
| Stalk Color |
| Stalk Diameter |
| Stalk texture |
| Stalk surface |
| Stalk Length |
| Special Properties |
| |

**Cap Characteristics ❖**

| Cap shape |
|---|
| Cap Color |
| Cap Diameter |
| Cap Texture |
| Cap Surface |
| Cap Length |
| Special Properties |
| Hymenium |

## Additional Notes

..........................................................
..........................................................
..........................................................
..........................................................
..........................................................
..........................................................
..........................................................
..........................................................
..........................................................
..........................................................
..........................................................

| *Species/Type* |
|---|
| |
| |
| |

| Name: | ❖ Weather condition |
|---|---|
| Location: | |
| Date: | |

## ❖ Type of Forest

| ❑ Deciduous | ❑ Tropical |
|---|---|
| ❑ Coniferous | ❑ Other |

## ❖ surrounding plant

| | |
|---|---|
| | |

**Stalk Characteristics** ❖

| Stalk shape |
|---|
| Stalk Color |
| Stalk Diameter |
| Stalk texture |
| Stalk surface |
| Stalk Length |
| Special Properties |
| |

**Cap Characteristics** ❖

| Cap shape |
|---|
| Cap Color |
| Cap Diameter |
| Cap Texture |
| Cap Surface |
| Cap Length |
| Special Properties |
| Hymenium |

## Additional Notes

## Species/Type

| Name: | ❖ Weather condition |
|---|---|
| Location: | |
| Date: | |

## ❖ Type of Forest

| | |
|---|---|
| ❑ Deciduous | ❑ Tropical |
| ❑ Coniferous | ❑ Other |

## ❖ surrounding plant

| | |
|---|---|
| | |
| | |

**Stalk Characteristics**

| |
|---|
| Stalk shape |
| Stalk Color |
| Stalk Diameter |
| Stalk texture |
| Stalk surface |
| Stalk Length |
| ❖ Special Properties |
| |

**Cap Characteristics**

| |
|---|
| Cap shape |
| Cap Color |
| Cap Diameter |
| Cap Texture |
| Cap Surface |
| Cap Length |
| ❖ Special Properties |
| Hymenium |

## Additional Notes

.......................................................
.......................................................
.......................................................
.......................................................
.......................................................
.......................................................
.......................................................
.......................................................
.......................................................
.......................................................
.......................................................
.......................................................

### *Species/Type*

| |
|---|
| |
| |

| Name: | ❖ Weather condition |
|---|---|
| Location: | |
| Date: | |

## ❖ Type of Forest

| ☐ Deciduous | ☐ Tropical |
|---|---|
| ☐ Coniferous | ☐ Other |

## ❖ surrounding plant

| | |
|---|---|
| | |

### Stalk Characteristics

| Stalk shape |
|---|
| Stalk Color |
| Stalk Diameter |
| Stalk texture |
| Stalk surface |
| Stalk Length |
| ❖ Special Properties |
| |

### Cap Characteristics

| Cap shape |
|---|
| Cap Color |
| Cap Diameter |
| Cap Texture |
| Cap Surface |
| Cap Length |
| ❖ Special Properties |
| Hymenium |

## Additional Notes

## Species/Type

| |
|---|
| |
| |

| Name: | ❖ Weather condition |
|---|---|
| Location: | |
| Date: | |

## ❖ Type of Forest

| ❏ Deciduous | ❏ Tropical |
|---|---|
| ❏ Coniferous | ❏ Other |

## ❖ surrounding plant

| | |
|---|---|
| | |

**Stalk Characteristics ❖**

| Stalk shape |
|---|
| Stalk Color |
| Stalk Diameter |
| Stalk texture |
| Stalk surface |
| Stalk Length |
| Special Properties |
| |

**Cap Characteristics ❖**

| Cap shape |
|---|
| Cap Color |
| Cap Diameter |
| Cap Texture |
| Cap Surface |
| Cap Length |
| Special Properties |
| Hymenium |

## Additional Notes

........................................
........................................
........................................
........................................
........................................
........................................
........................................
........................................
........................................
........................................
........................................

### Species/Type

| | |
|---|---|
| Name: | ❖ Weather condition |
| Location: | |
| Date: | |

| ❖ Type of Forest | | ❖ surrounding plant |
|---|---|---|
| ❑ Deciduous | ❑ Tropical | |
| ❑ Coniferous | ❑ Other | |

| *Stalk Characteristics* ❖ | | *Cap Characteristics* ❖ | |
|---|---|---|---|
| | Stalk shape | | Cap shape |
| | Stalk Color | | Cap Color |
| | Stalk Diameter | | Cap Diameter |
| | Stalk texture | | Cap Texture |
| | Stalk surface | | Cap Surface |
| | Stalk Length | | Cap Length |
| | Special Properties | | Special Properties |
| | | | Hymenium |

## Additional Notes

| *Species/Type* |
|---|
| |
| |
| |

| Name: | ❖ Weather condition |
|---|---|
| Location: | |
| Date: | |

## ❖ Type of Forest

| ❑ Deciduous | ❑ Tropical |
|---|---|
| ❑ Coniferous | ❑ Other |

## ❖ surrounding plant

| | |
|---|---|
| | |

**Stalk Characteristics**

| Stalk shape |
|---|
| Stalk Color |
| Stalk Diameter |
| Stalk texture |
| Stalk surface |
| Stalk Length |
| ❖ Special Properties |
| |

**Cap Characteristics**

| Cap shape |
|---|
| Cap Color |
| Cap Diameter |
| Cap Texture |
| Cap Surface |
| Cap Length |
| ❖ Special Properties |
| Hymenium |

## Additional Notes

.................................................
.................................................
.................................................
.................................................
.................................................
.................................................
.................................................
.................................................
.................................................
.................................................
.................................................
.................................................

## Species/Type

| |
|---|
| |
| |

| Name: | ❖ Weather condition |
|---|---|
| Location: | |
| Date: | |

## ❖ Type of Forest

| | |
|---|---|
| ❑ Deciduous | ❑ Tropical |
| ❑ Coniferous | ❑ Other |

## ❖ surrounding plant

| | |
|---|---|
| | |
| | |

**Stalk Characteristics**

| ❖ | |
|---|---|
| | Stalk shape |
| | Stalk Color |
| | Stalk Diameter |
| | Stalk texture |
| | Stalk surface |
| | Stalk Length |
| | Special Properties |
| | |

**Cap Characteristics**

| ❖ | |
|---|---|
| | Cap shape |
| | Cap Color |
| | Cap Diameter |
| | Cap Texture |
| | Cap Surface |
| | Cap Length |
| | Special Properties |
| | Hymenium |

## Additional Notes

## Species/Type

| Name: | ❖ Weather condition |
|---|---|
| Location: | |
| Date: | |

## ❖ Type of Forest

| ❏ Deciduous | ❏ Tropical |
|---|---|
| ❏ Coniferous | ❏ Other |

## ❖ surrounding plant

| | |
|---|---|
| | |

**Stalk Characteristics**

| Stalk shape |
|---|
| Stalk Color |
| Stalk Diameter |
| Stalk texture |
| Stalk surface |
| Stalk Length |
| ❖ Special Properties |
| |

**Cap Characteristics**

| Cap shape |
|---|
| Cap Color |
| Cap Diameter |
| Cap Texture |
| Cap Surface |
| Cap Length |
| ❖ Special Properties |
| Hymenium |

## Additional Notes

## *Species/Type*

| Name: | | ❖ Weather condition |
|---|---|---|
| Location: | | |
| Date: | | |

## ❖ Type of Forest

| ❑ Deciduous | ❑ Tropical |
|---|---|
| ❑ Coniferous | ❑ Other |

## ❖ surrounding plant

| | |
|---|---|
| | |

### Stalk Characteristics

| Stalk shape |
|---|
| Stalk Color |
| Stalk Diameter |
| Stalk texture |
| Stalk surface |
| Stalk Length |
| ❖ Special Properties |
| |

### Cap Characteristics

| Cap shape |
|---|
| Cap Color |
| Cap Diameter |
| Cap Texture |
| Cap Surface |
| Cap Length |
| ❖ Special Properties |
| Hymenium |

## Additional Notes

## Species/Type

| Name: | ❖ Weather condition |
|---|---|
| Location: | |
| Date: | |

## ❖ Type of Forest

| ☐ Deciduous | ☐ Tropical |
|---|---|
| ☐ Coniferous | ☐ Other |

## ❖ surrounding plant

| | |
|---|---|
| | |

## Stalk Characteristics

| Stalk shape |
|---|
| Stalk Color |
| Stalk Diameter |
| Stalk texture |
| Stalk surface |
| Stalk Length |
| ❖ Special Properties |
| |

## Cap Characteristics

| Cap shape |
|---|
| Cap Color |
| Cap Diameter |
| Cap Texture |
| Cap Surface |
| Cap Length |
| ❖ Special Properties |
| Hymenium |

## Additional Notes

........................................
........................................
........................................
........................................
........................................
........................................
........................................
........................................
........................................
........................................
........................................

## Species/Type

| |
|---|
| |
| |

| Name: | ❖ Weather condition |
|---|---|
| Location: | |
| Date: | |

## ❖ Type of Forest

| ☐ Deciduous | ☐ Tropical |
|---|---|
| ☐ Coniferous | ☐ Other |

## ❖ surrounding plant

| | |
|---|---|
| | |

**Stalk Characteristics**

| Stalk shape |
|---|
| Stalk Color |
| Stalk Diameter |
| Stalk texture |
| Stalk surface |
| Stalk Length |
| ❖ Special Properties |
| |

**Cap Characteristics**

| Cap shape |
|---|
| Cap Color |
| Cap Diameter |
| Cap Texture |
| Cap Surface |
| Cap Length |
| ❖ Special Properties |
| Hymenium |

## Additional Notes

## *Species/Type*

| Name: | ❖ Weather condition |
| Location: | |
| Date: | |

| ❖ Type of Forest | | ❖ surrounding plant | |
|---|---|---|---|
| ❏ Deciduous | ❏ Tropical | | |
| ❏ Coniferous | ❏ Other | | |

**Stalk Characteristics**

| Stalk shape | |
|---|---|
| Stalk Color | |
| Stalk Diameter | |
| Stalk texture | |
| Stalk surface | |
| Stalk Length | |
| ❖ Special Properties | |

**Cap Characteristics**

| Cap shape | |
|---|---|
| Cap Color | |
| Cap Diameter | |
| Cap Texture | |
| Cap Surface | |
| Cap Length | |
| ❖ Special Properties | |
| Hymenium | |

Additional Notes

........................................................
........................................................
........................................................
........................................................
........................................................
........................................................
........................................................
........................................................
........................................................
........................................................
........................................................

| *Species/Type* |
|---|
| |
| |
| |

| Name: | ❖ Weather condition |
|---|---|
| Location: | |
| Date: | |

## ❖ Type of Forest

| ❑ Deciduous | ❑ Tropical |
|---|---|
| ❑ Coniferous | ❑ Other |

## ❖ surrounding plant

| | |
|---|---|
| | |

| *Stalk Characteristics* | |
|---|---|
| | Stalk shape |
| | Stalk Color |
| | Stalk Diameter |
| | Stalk texture |
| | Stalk surface |
| | Stalk Length |
| ❖ | Special Properties |
| | |

| *Cap Characteristics* | |
|---|---|
| | Cap shape |
| | Cap Color |
| | Cap Diameter |
| | Cap Texture |
| | Cap Surface |
| | Cap Length |
| ❖ | Special Properties |
| | Hymenium |

## Additional Notes

..........................................................
..........................................................
..........................................................
..........................................................
..........................................................
..........................................................
..........................................................
..........................................................
..........................................................
..........................................................
..........................................................

### *Species/Type*

| |
|---|
| |
| |

| Name: | ❖ Weather condition |
|---|---|
| Location: | |
| Date: | |

| ❖ Type of Forest | | ❖ surrounding plant | |
|---|---|---|---|
| ☐ Deciduous | ☐ Tropical | | |
| ☐ Coniferous | ☐ Other | | |

| Stalk Characteristics | | Cap Characteristics | |
|---|---|---|---|
| | Stalk shape | | Cap shape |
| | Stalk Color | | Cap Color |
| | Stalk Diameter | | Cap Diameter |
| | Stalk texture | | Cap Texture |
| | Stalk surface | | Cap Surface |
| | Stalk Length | | Cap Length |
| ❖ | Special Properties | ❖ | Special Properties |
| | | | Hymenium |

## Additional Notes

...........................................................
...........................................................
...........................................................
...........................................................
...........................................................
...........................................................
...........................................................
...........................................................
...........................................................
...........................................................
...........................................................

| *Species/Type* |
|---|
| |
| |
| |

| Name: | ❖ Weather condition |
| --- | --- |
| Location: | |
| Date: | |

| ❖ Type of Forest | | ❖ surrounding plant | |
| --- | --- | --- | --- |
| ❑ Deciduous | ❑ Tropical | | |
| ❑ Coniferous | ❑ Other | | |

| *Stalk Characteristics* ❖ | Stalk shape |
| --- | --- |
| | Stalk Color |
| | Stalk Diameter |
| | Stalk texture |
| | Stalk surface |
| | Stalk Length |
| | Special Properties |
| | |

| *Cap Characteristics* ❖ | Cap shape |
| --- | --- |
| | Cap Color |
| | Cap Diameter |
| | Cap Texture |
| | Cap Surface |
| | Cap Length |
| | Special Properties |
| | Hymenium |

Additional Notes

| Species/Type |
| --- |
| |
| |
| |

| Name: | ❖ Weather condition |
|---|---|
| Location: | |
| Date: | |

## ❖ Type of Forest

| ☐ Deciduous | ☐ Tropical |
|---|---|
| ☐ Coniferous | ☐ Other |

## ❖ surrounding plant

| | |
|---|---|
| | |

**Stalk Characteristics**

| Stalk shape | |
|---|---|
| Stalk Color | |
| Stalk Diameter | |
| Stalk texture | |
| Stalk surface | |
| Stalk Length | |
| ❖ Special Properties | |

**Cap Characteristics**

| Cap shape | |
|---|---|
| Cap Color | |
| Cap Diameter | |
| Cap Texture | |
| Cap Surface | |
| Cap Length | |
| ❖ Special Properties | |
| Hymenium | |

## Additional Notes

...........................................................
...........................................................
...........................................................
...........................................................
...........................................................
...........................................................
...........................................................
...........................................................
...........................................................
...........................................................
...........................................................
...........................................................

| *Species/Type* |
|---|
| |
| |
| |

| Name: | ❖ Weather condition |
|---|---|
| Location: | |
| Date: | |

## ❖ Type of Forest

| ❑ Deciduous | ❑ Tropical |
|---|---|
| ❑ Coniferous | ❑ Other |

## ❖ surrounding plant

| | |
|---|---|
| | |

### Stalk Characteristics

| Stalk shape |
|---|
| Stalk Color |
| Stalk Diameter |
| Stalk texture |
| Stalk surface |
| Stalk Length |
| ❖ Special Properties |
| |

### Cap Characteristics

| Cap shape |
|---|
| Cap Color |
| Cap Diameter |
| Cap Texture |
| Cap Surface |
| Cap Length |
| ❖ Special Properties |
| Hymenium |

## Additional Notes

## Species/Type

| Name: | ❖ Weather condition |
|---|---|
| Location: | |
| Date: | |

## ❖ Type of Forest

| ❑ Deciduous | ❑ Tropical |
|---|---|
| ❑ Coniferous | ❑ Other |

## ❖ surrounding plant

| | |
|---|---|
| | |

**Stalk Characteristics**

| Stalk shape |
|---|
| Stalk Color |
| Stalk Diameter |
| Stalk texture |
| Stalk surface |
| Stalk Length |
| ❖ Special Properties |
| |

**Cap Characteristics**

| Cap shape |
|---|
| Cap Color |
| Cap Diameter |
| Cap Texture |
| Cap Surface |
| Cap Length |
| ❖ Special Properties |
| Hymenium |

## Additional Notes

........................................................
........................................................
........................................................
........................................................
........................................................
........................................................
........................................................
........................................................
........................................................
........................................................

### Species/Type

| |
|---|
| |
| |

| Name: | ❖ Weather condition |
| Location: | |
| Date: | |

## ❖ Type of Forest

| ☐ Deciduous | ☐ Tropical |
| ☐ Coniferous | ☐ Other |

## ❖ surrounding plant

| | |
| | |

**Stalk Characteristics**

| Stalk shape |
| Stalk Color |
| Stalk Diameter |
| Stalk texture |
| Stalk surface |
| Stalk Length |
| ❖ Special Properties |
| |

**Cap Characteristics**

| Cap shape |
| Cap Color |
| Cap Diameter |
| Cap Texture |
| Cap Surface |
| Cap Length |
| ❖ Special Properties |
| Hymenium |

## Additional Notes

## Species/Type

| Name: | ❖ Weather condition |
|---|---|
| Location: | |
| Date: | |

## ❖ Type of Forest

| | |
|---|---|
| ❑ Deciduous | ❑ Tropical |
| ❑ Coniferous | ❑ Other |

## ❖ surrounding plant

| | |
|---|---|
| | |
| | |

**Stalk Characteristics**

| Stalk shape |
|---|
| Stalk Color |
| Stalk Diameter |
| Stalk texture |
| Stalk surface |
| Stalk Length |
| ❖ Special Properties |
| |

**Cap Characteristics**

| Cap shape |
|---|
| Cap Color |
| Cap Diameter |
| Cap Texture |
| Cap Surface |
| Cap Length |
| ❖ Special Properties |
| Hymenium |

## Additional Notes

..................................................
..................................................
..................................................
..................................................
..................................................
..................................................
..................................................
..................................................
..................................................
..................................................
..................................................

## Species/Type

| |
|---|
| |
| |

| Name: | ❖ Weather condition |
| Location: | |
| Date: | |

## ❖ Type of Forest

| ☐ Deciduous | ☐ Tropical |
|---|---|
| ☐ Coniferous | ☐ Other |

## ❖ surrounding plant

| | |
|---|---|
| | |

**Stalk Characteristics**

| Stalk shape |
|---|
| Stalk Color |
| Stalk Diameter |
| Stalk texture |
| Stalk surface |
| Stalk Length |
| ❖ Special Properties |
| |

**Cap Characteristics**

| Cap shape |
|---|
| Cap Color |
| Cap Diameter |
| Cap Texture |
| Cap Surface |
| Cap Length |
| ❖ Special Properties |
| Hymenium |

## Additional Notes

## *Species/Type*

| Name: | ❖ Weather condition |
|---|---|
| Location: | |
| Date: | |

## ❖ Type of Forest

| | |
|---|---|
| ❑ Deciduous | ❑ Tropical |
| ❑ Coniferous | ❑ Other |

## ❖ surrounding plant

| | |
|---|---|
| | |
| | |

**Stalk Characteristics**

| | |
|---|---|
| Stalk shape | |
| Stalk Color | |
| Stalk Diameter | |
| Stalk texture | |
| Stalk surface | |
| Stalk Length | |
| ❖ Special Properties | |
| | |

**Cap Characteristics**

| | |
|---|---|
| Cap shape | |
| Cap Color | |
| Cap Diameter | |
| Cap Texture | |
| Cap Surface | |
| Cap Length | |
| ❖ Special Properties | |
| Hymenium | |

## Additional Notes

..........................................................
..........................................................
..........................................................
..........................................................
..........................................................
..........................................................
..........................................................
..........................................................
..........................................................

## Species/Type

| |
|---|
| |
| |

| Name: | ❖ Weather condition |
|---|---|
| Location: | |
| Date: | |

## ❖ Type of Forest

| ☐ Deciduous | ☐ Tropical |
|---|---|
| ☐ Coniferous | ☐ Other |

## ❖ surrounding plant

| | |
|---|---|
| | |

**Stalk Characteristics**

| Stalk shape |
|---|
| Stalk Color |
| Stalk Diameter |
| Stalk texture |
| Stalk surface |
| Stalk Length |
| ❖ Special Properties |
| |

**Cap Characteristics**

| Cap shape |
|---|
| Cap Color |
| Cap Diameter |
| Cap Texture |
| Cap Surface |
| Cap Length |
| ❖ Special Properties |
| Hymenium |

## Additional Notes

## Species/Type

| Name: | ❖ Weather condition |
|---|---|
| Location: | |
| Date: | |

## ❖ Type of Forest

| ❏ Deciduous | ❏ Tropical |
|---|---|
| ❏ Coniferous | ❏ Other |

## ❖ surrounding plant

| | |
|---|---|
| | |

**Stalk Characteristics**
❖

| Stalk shape |
|---|
| Stalk Color |
| Stalk Diameter |
| Stalk texture |
| Stalk surface |
| Stalk Length |
| Special Properties |
| |

**Cap Characteristics**
❖

| Cap shape |
|---|
| Cap Color |
| Cap Diameter |
| Cap Texture |
| Cap Surface |
| Cap Length |
| Special Properties |
| Hymenium |

## Additional Notes

......................................................
......................................................
......................................................
......................................................
......................................................
......................................................
......................................................
......................................................
......................................................
......................................................
......................................................

## *Species/Type*

| |
|---|
| |
| |

| Name: | ❖ Weather condition |
|---|---|
| Location: | |
| Date: | |

## ❖ Type of Forest

| ❑ Deciduous | ❑ Tropical |
|---|---|
| ❑ Coniferous | ❑ Other |

## ❖ surrounding plant

| | |
|---|---|
| | |

**Stalk Characteristics**

| Stalk shape |
|---|
| Stalk Color |
| Stalk Diameter |
| Stalk texture |
| Stalk surface |
| Stalk Length |
| ❖ Special Properties |
| |

**Cap Characteristics**

| Cap shape |
|---|
| Cap Color |
| Cap Diameter |
| Cap Texture |
| Cap Surface |
| Cap Length |
| ❖ Special Properties |
| Hymenium |

## Additional Notes

## Species/Type

| |
|---|
| |
| |

| Name: | ❖ Weather condition |
|---|---|
| Location: | |
| Date: | |

## ❖ Type of Forest

| ❏ Deciduous | ❏ Tropical |
|---|---|
| ❏ Coniferous | ❏ Other |

## ❖ surrounding plant

| | |
|---|---|
| | |

**Stalk Characteristics** ❖

| Stalk shape |
|---|
| Stalk Color |
| Stalk Diameter |
| Stalk texture |
| Stalk surface |
| Stalk Length |
| Special Properties |
| |

**Cap Characteristics** ❖

| Cap shape |
|---|
| Cap Color |
| Cap Diameter |
| Cap Texture |
| Cap Surface |
| Cap Length |
| Special Properties |
| Hymenium |

## Additional Notes

## Species/Type

| Name: | ❖ Weather condition |
|---|---|
| Location: | |
| Date: | |

## ❖ Type of Forest

| ❏ Deciduous | ❏ Tropical |
|---|---|
| ❏ Coniferous | ❏ Other |

## ❖ surrounding plant

| | |
|---|---|
| | |

**Stalk Characteristics** ❖

| Stalk shape |
|---|
| Stalk Color |
| Stalk Diameter |
| Stalk texture |
| Stalk surface |
| Stalk Length |
| Special Properties |
| |

**Cap Characteristics** ❖

| Cap shape |
|---|
| Cap Color |
| Cap Diameter |
| Cap Texture |
| Cap Surface |
| Cap Length |
| Special Properties |
| Hymenium |

## Additional Notes

## Species/Type

| Name: | ❖ Weather condition |
|---|---|
| Location: | |
| Date: | |

| ❖ Type of Forest | | ❖ surrounding plant | |
|---|---|---|---|
| ☐ Deciduous | ☐ Tropical | | |
| ☐ Coniferous | ☐ Other | | |

| Stalk Characteristics | | Cap Characteristics | |
|---|---|---|---|
| | Stalk shape | | Cap shape |
| | Stalk Color | | Cap Color |
| | Stalk Diameter | | Cap Diameter |
| | Stalk texture | | Cap Texture |
| | Stalk surface | | Cap Surface |
| | Stalk Length | | Cap Length |
| ❖ | Special Properties | ❖ | Special Properties |
| | | | Hymenium |

## Additional Notes

........................................................
........................................................
........................................................
........................................................
........................................................
........................................................
........................................................
........................................................
........................................................
........................................................
........................................................

| *Species/Type* |
|---|
| |
| |
| |

| Name: | ❖ Weather condition |
|---|---|
| Location: | |
| Date: | |

## ❖ Type of Forest

| ☐ Deciduous | ☐ Tropical |
|---|---|
| ☐ Coniferous | ☐ Other |

## ❖ surrounding plant

| | |
|---|---|
| | |

**Stalk Characteristics**

| Stalk shape |
|---|
| Stalk Color |
| Stalk Diameter |
| Stalk texture |
| Stalk surface |
| Stalk Length |
| ❖ Special Properties |
| |

**Cap Characteristics**

| Cap shape |
|---|
| Cap Color |
| Cap Diameter |
| Cap Texture |
| Cap Surface |
| Cap Length |
| ❖ Special Properties |
| Hymenium |

## Additional Notes

## Species/Type

| Name: | ❖ Weather condition |
|---|---|
| Location: | |
| Date: | |

### ❖ Type of Forest

| ❏ Deciduous | ❏ Tropical |
|---|---|
| ❏ Coniferous | ❏ Other |

### ❖ surrounding plant

| | |
|---|---|
| | |

**Stalk Characteristics** ❖

| Stalk shape |
|---|
| Stalk Color |
| Stalk Diameter |
| Stalk texture |
| Stalk surface |
| Stalk Length |
| Special Properties |

**Cap Characteristics** ❖

| Cap shape |
|---|
| Cap Color |
| Cap Diameter |
| Cap Texture |
| Cap Surface |
| Cap Length |
| Special Properties |
| Hymenium |

### Additional Notes

### *Species/Type*

| |
|---|
| |
| |

| Name: | ❖ Weather condition |
| Location: | |
| Date: | |

## ❖ Type of Forest

| ❏ Deciduous | ❏ Tropical |
| ❏ Coniferous | ❏ Other |

## ❖ surrounding plant

| | |
| | |

**Stalk Characteristics** ❖

| Stalk shape |
| Stalk Color |
| Stalk Diameter |
| Stalk texture |
| Stalk surface |
| Stalk Length |
| Special Properties |
| |

**Cap Characteristics** ❖

| Cap shape |
| Cap Color |
| Cap Diameter |
| Cap Texture |
| Cap Surface |
| Cap Length |
| Special Properties |
| Hymenium |

## Additional Notes

## *Species/Type*

| Name: | ❖ Weather condition |
|---|---|
| Location: | |
| Date: | |

## ❖ Type of Forest

| ☐ Deciduous | ☐ Tropical |
|---|---|
| ☐ Coniferous | ☐ Other |

## ❖ surrounding plant

| | |
|---|---|
| | |

**Stalk Characteristics**

| Stalk shape |
|---|
| Stalk Color |
| Stalk Diameter |
| Stalk texture |
| Stalk surface |
| Stalk Length |
| ❖ Special Properties |
| |

**Cap Characteristics**

| Cap shape |
|---|
| Cap Color |
| Cap Diameter |
| Cap Texture |
| Cap Surface |
| Cap Length |
| ❖ Special Properties |
| Hymenium |

## Additional Notes

## Species/Type

| Name: | ❖ Weather condition |
|-------|---------------------|
| Location: | |
| Date: | |

## ❖ Type of Forest

| ❑ Deciduous | ❑ Tropical |
|-------------|------------|
| ❑ Coniferous | ❑ Other |

## ❖ surrounding plant

| | |
|--|--|
| | |

**Stalk Characteristics** ❖

| Stalk shape |
|-------------|
| Stalk Color |
| Stalk Diameter |
| Stalk texture |
| Stalk surface |
| Stalk Length |
| Special Properties |
| |

**Cap Characteristics** ❖

| Cap shape |
|-----------|
| Cap Color |
| Cap Diameter |
| Cap Texture |
| Cap Surface |
| Cap Length |
| Special Properties |
| Hymenium |

## Additional Notes

........................................
........................................
........................................
........................................
........................................
........................................
........................................
........................................
........................................
........................................

### Species/Type

| |
|--|
| |
| |

| Name: | ❖ Weather condition |
|---|---|
| Location: | |
| Date: | |

## ❖ Type of Forest

| ❑ Deciduous | ❑ Tropical |
|---|---|
| ❑ Coniferous | ❑ Other |

## ❖ surrounding plant

| | |
|---|---|
| | |

**Stalk Characteristics**

| Stalk shape |
|---|
| Stalk Color |
| Stalk Diameter |
| Stalk texture |
| Stalk surface |
| Stalk Length |
| ❖ Special Properties |
| |

**Cap Characteristics**

| Cap shape |
|---|
| Cap Color |
| Cap Diameter |
| Cap Texture |
| Cap Surface |
| Cap Length |
| ❖ Special Properties |
| Hymenium |

## Additional Notes

...................................................................
...................................................................
...................................................................
...................................................................
...................................................................
...................................................................
...................................................................
...................................................................
...................................................................
...................................................................
...................................................................
...................................................................
...................................................................

### Species/Type

| |
|---|
| |
| |

| Name: | ❖ Weather condition |
|---|---|
| Location: | |
| Date: | |

| ❖ Type of Forest | | ❖ surrounding plant | |
|---|---|---|---|
| ❑ Deciduous | ❑ Tropical | | |
| ❑ Coniferous | ❑ Other | | |

| **Stalk Characteristics** | Stalk shape | **Cap Characteristics** | Cap shape |
|---|---|---|---|
| | Stalk Color | | Cap Color |
| | Stalk Diameter | | Cap Diameter |
| | Stalk texture | | Cap Texture |
| | Stalk surface | | Cap Surface |
| | Stalk Length | | Cap Length |
| ❖ | Special Properties | ❖ | Special Properties |
| | | | Hymenium |

## Additional Notes

..........................................................
..........................................................
..........................................................
..........................................................
..........................................................
..........................................................
..........................................................
..........................................................
..........................................................

| *Species/Type* |
|---|
| |
| |
| |

| Name: | ❖ Weather condition |
|---|---|
| Location: | |
| Date: | |

## ❖ Type of Forest

| ❑ Deciduous | ❑ Tropical |
|---|---|
| ❑ Coniferous | ❑ Other |

## ❖ surrounding plant

| | |
|---|---|
| | |

**Stalk Characteristics**

| Stalk shape |
|---|
| Stalk Color |
| Stalk Diameter |
| Stalk texture |
| Stalk surface |
| Stalk Length |
| ❖ Special Properties |
| |

**Cap Characteristics**

| Cap shape |
|---|
| Cap Color |
| Cap Diameter |
| Cap Texture |
| Cap Surface |
| Cap Length |
| ❖ Special Properties |
| Hymenium |

## Additional Notes

..............................................
..............................................
..............................................
..............................................
..............................................
..............................................
..............................................
..............................................
..............................................
..............................................
..............................................
..............................................

### Species/Type

| |
|---|
| |
| |

| | |
|---|---|
| Name: | ❖ **Weather condition** |
| Location: | |
| Date: | |

## ❖ Type of Forest

| | |
|---|---|
| ❑ Deciduous | ❑ Tropical |
| ❑ Coniferous | ❑ Other |

## ❖ surrounding plant

| | |
|---|---|
| | |
| | |

**Stalk Characteristics**

| |
|---|
| Stalk shape |
| Stalk Color |
| Stalk Diameter |
| Stalk texture |
| Stalk surface |
| Stalk Length |
| ❖ Special Properties |
| |

**Cap Characteristics**

| |
|---|
| Cap shape |
| Cap Color |
| Cap Diameter |
| Cap Texture |
| Cap Surface |
| Cap Length |
| ❖ Special Properties |
| Hymenium |

## Additional Notes

........................................................
........................................................
........................................................
........................................................
........................................................
........................................................
........................................................
........................................................
........................................................
........................................................
........................................................

## *Species/Type*

| |
|---|
| |
| |
| |

| Name: | ❖ Weather condition |
|---|---|
| Location: | |
| Date: | |

## ❖ Type of Forest

| ❑ Deciduous | ❑ Tropical |
|---|---|
| ❑ Coniferous | ❑ Other |

## ❖ surrounding plant

| | |
|---|---|
| | |

**Stalk Characteristics**

| Stalk shape |
|---|
| Stalk Color |
| Stalk Diameter |
| Stalk texture |
| Stalk surface |
| Stalk Length |
| ❖ Special Properties |
| |

**Cap Characteristics**

| Cap shape |
|---|
| Cap Color |
| Cap Diameter |
| Cap Texture |
| Cap Surface |
| Cap Length |
| ❖ Special Properties |
| Hymenium |

## Additional Notes

........................................
........................................
........................................
........................................
........................................
........................................
........................................
........................................
........................................
........................................
........................................

### Species/Type

| |
|---|
| |
| |

| Name: | ❖ Weather condition |
|---|---|
| Location: | |
| Date: | |

## ❖ Type of Forest

| ☐ Deciduous | ☐ Tropical |
|---|---|
| ☐ Coniferous | ☐ Other |

## ❖ surrounding plant

| | |
|---|---|
| | |

**Stalk Characteristics** ❖

| Stalk shape |
|---|
| Stalk Color |
| Stalk Diameter |
| Stalk texture |
| Stalk surface |
| Stalk Length |
| Special Properties |
| |

**Cap Characteristics** ❖

| Cap shape |
|---|
| Cap Color |
| Cap Diameter |
| Cap Texture |
| Cap Surface |
| Cap Length |
| Special Properties |
| Hymenium |

## Additional Notes

## *Species/Type*

| Name: | ❖ Weather condition |
|---|---|
| Location: | |
| Date: | |

## ❖ Type of Forest

| ☐ Deciduous | ☐ Tropical |
|---|---|
| ☐ Coniferous | ☐ Other |

## ❖ surrounding plant

| | |
|---|---|
| | |

**Stalk Characteristics**

| Stalk shape |
|---|
| Stalk Color |
| Stalk Diameter |
| Stalk texture |
| Stalk surface |
| Stalk Length |
| ❖ Special Properties |
| |

**Cap Characteristics**

| Cap shape |
|---|
| Cap Color |
| Cap Diameter |
| Cap Texture |
| Cap Surface |
| Cap Length |
| ❖ Special Properties |
| Hymenium |

## Additional Notes

......................................
......................................
......................................
......................................
......................................
......................................
......................................
......................................
......................................
......................................
......................................

### Species/Type

| Name: | ❖ Weather condition |
|---|---|
| Location: | |
| Date: | |

### ❖ Type of Forest

| ❑ Deciduous | ❑ Tropical |
|---|---|
| ❑ Coniferous | ❑ Other |

### ❖ surrounding plant

| | |
|---|---|
| | |

**Stalk Characteristics**

| Stalk shape |
|---|
| Stalk Color |
| Stalk Diameter |
| Stalk texture |
| Stalk surface |
| Stalk Length |
| ❖ Special Properties |
| |

**Cap Characteristics**

| Cap shape |
|---|
| Cap Color |
| Cap Diameter |
| Cap Texture |
| Cap Surface |
| Cap Length |
| ❖ Special Properties |
| Hymenium |

### Additional Notes

### Species/Type

| |
|---|
| |
| |

| Name: | ❖ Weather condition |
|---|---|
| Location: | |
| Date: | |

## ❖ Type of Forest

| ☐ Deciduous | ☐ Tropical |
|---|---|
| ☐ Coniferous | ☐ Other |

## ❖ surrounding plant

| | |
|---|---|
| | |

### Stalk Characteristics ❖

| Stalk shape | |
|---|---|
| Stalk Color | |
| Stalk Diameter | |
| Stalk texture | |
| Stalk surface | |
| Stalk Length | |
| Special Properties | |

### Cap Characteristics ❖

| Cap shape | |
|---|---|
| Cap Color | |
| Cap Diameter | |
| Cap Texture | |
| Cap Surface | |
| Cap Length | |
| Special Properties | |
| Hymenium | |

## Additional Notes

## Species/Type

| Name: | ❖ Weather condition |
|---|---|
| Location: | |
| Date: | |

## ❖ Type of Forest

| ❏ Deciduous | ❏ Tropical |
|---|---|
| ❏ Coniferous | ❏ Other |

## ❖ surrounding plant

| | |
|---|---|
| | |

**Stalk Characteristics** ❖

| Stalk shape |
|---|
| Stalk Color |
| Stalk Diameter |
| Stalk texture |
| Stalk surface |
| Stalk Length |
| Special Properties |
| |

**Cap Characteristics** ❖

| Cap shape |
|---|
| Cap Color |
| Cap Diameter |
| Cap Texture |
| Cap Surface |
| Cap Length |
| Special Properties |
| Hymenium |

## Additional Notes

## Species/Type

| Name: | ❖ Weather condition |
|---|---|
| Location: | |
| Date: | |

| ❖ Type of Forest | ❖ surrounding plant |
|---|---|

### ❖ Type of Forest

| ❏ Deciduous | ❏ Tropical |
|---|---|
| ❏ Coniferous | ❏ Other |

### ❖ surrounding plant

| | |
|---|---|
| | |

**Stalk Characteristics**

| Stalk shape |
|---|
| Stalk Color |
| Stalk Diameter |
| Stalk texture |
| Stalk surface |
| Stalk Length |
| ❖ Special Properties |
| |

**Cap Characteristics**

| Cap shape |
|---|
| Cap Color |
| Cap Diameter |
| Cap Texture |
| Cap Surface |
| Cap Length |
| ❖ Special Properties |
| Hymenium |

### Additional Notes

...................................................
...................................................
...................................................
...................................................
...................................................
...................................................
...................................................
...................................................
...................................................
...................................................

### Species/Type

| |
|---|
| |
| |

| Name: | ❖ Weather condition |
|---|---|
| Location: | |
| Date: | |

| ❖ Type of Forest | | | ❖ surrounding plant | |
|---|---|---|---|---|
| ❑ Deciduous | ❑ Tropical | | | |
| ❑ Coniferous | ❑ Other | | | |

**Stalk Characteristics** ❖

| Stalk shape |
|---|
| Stalk Color |
| Stalk Diameter |
| Stalk texture |
| Stalk surface |
| Stalk Length |
| Special Properties |
| |

**Cap Characteristics** ❖

| Cap shape |
|---|
| Cap Color |
| Cap Diameter |
| Cap Texture |
| Cap Surface |
| Cap Length |
| Special Properties |
| Hymenium |

## Additional Notes

...........................................................
...........................................................
...........................................................
...........................................................
...........................................................
...........................................................
...........................................................
...........................................................
...........................................................
...........................................................

### Species/Type
| |
|---|
| |
| |

| Name: | ❖ Weather condition |
|---|---|
| Location: | |
| Date: | |

## ❖ Type of Forest

| ☐ Deciduous | ☐ Tropical |
|---|---|
| ☐ Coniferous | ☐ Other |

## ❖ surrounding plant

| | |
|---|---|
| | |

**Stalk Characteristics**

| Stalk shape |
|---|
| Stalk Color |
| Stalk Diameter |
| Stalk texture |
| Stalk surface |
| Stalk Length |
| ❖ Special Properties |
| |

**Cap Characteristics**

| Cap shape |
|---|
| Cap Color |
| Cap Diameter |
| Cap Texture |
| Cap Surface |
| Cap Length |
| ❖ Special Properties |
| Hymenium |

## Additional Notes

## *Species/Type*

| |
|---|
| |
| |

| Name: | ❖ Weather condition |
|---|---|
| Location: | |
| Date: | |

| ❖ Type of Forest | | ❖ surrounding plant | |
|---|---|---|---|
| ❑ Deciduous | ❑ Tropical | | |
| ❑ Coniferous | ❑ Other | | |

**Stalk Characteristics** ❖

| Stalk shape |
|---|
| Stalk Color |
| Stalk Diameter |
| Stalk texture |
| Stalk surface |
| Stalk Length |
| Special Properties |
| |

**Cap Characteristics** ❖

| Cap shape |
|---|
| Cap Color |
| Cap Diameter |
| Cap Texture |
| Cap Surface |
| Cap Length |
| Special Properties |
| Hymenium |

## Additional Notes

## Species/Type

| Name: | ❖ Weather condition |
|---|---|
| Location: | |
| Date: | |

| ❖ Type of Forest | | ❖ surrounding plant | |
|---|---|---|---|
| ❏ Deciduous | ❏ Tropical | | |
| ❏ Coniferous | ❏ Other | | |

| *Stalk Characteristics* | | | *Cap Characteristics* | |
|---|---|---|---|---|
| | Stalk shape | | | Cap shape |
| | Stalk Color | | | Cap Color |
| | Stalk Diameter | | | Cap Diameter |
| | Stalk texture | | | Cap Texture |
| | Stalk surface | | | Cap Surface |
| | Stalk Length | | | Cap Length |
| ❖ | Special Properties | | ❖ | Special Properties |
| | | | | Hymenium |

## Additional Notes

.................................................
.................................................
.................................................
.................................................
.................................................
.................................................
.................................................
.................................................
.................................................
.................................................
.................................................

| *Species/Type* |
|---|
| |
| |
| |

| Name: | ❖ Weather condition |
| Location: | |
| Date: | |

| ❖ Type of Forest | | ❖ surrounding plant | |
|---|---|---|---|
| ❑ Deciduous | ❑ Tropical | | |
| ❑ Coniferous | ❑ Other | | |

**Stalk Characteristics** ❖

| Stalk shape |
|---|
| Stalk Color |
| Stalk Diameter |
| Stalk texture |
| Stalk surface |
| Stalk Length |
| Special Properties |
| |

**Cap Characteristics** ❖

| Cap shape |
|---|
| Cap Color |
| Cap Diameter |
| Cap Texture |
| Cap Surface |
| Cap Length |
| Special Properties |
| Hymenium |

## Additional Notes

................................................
................................................
................................................
................................................
................................................
................................................
................................................
................................................
................................................
................................................
................................................

| *Species/Type* |
|---|
| |
| |
| |

| Name: | ❖ Weather condition |
|---|---|
| Location: | |
| Date: | |

## ❖ Type of Forest

| ❑ Deciduous | ❑ Tropical |
|---|---|
| ❑ Coniferous | ❑ Other |

## ❖ surrounding plant

| | |
|---|---|
| | |

**Stalk Characteristics**

| Stalk shape |
|---|
| Stalk Color |
| Stalk Diameter |
| Stalk texture |
| Stalk surface |
| Stalk Length |
| ❖ Special Properties |
| |

**Cap Characteristics**

| Cap shape |
|---|
| Cap Color |
| Cap Diameter |
| Cap Texture |
| Cap Surface |
| Cap Length |
| ❖ Special Properties |
| Hymenium |

## Additional Notes

## *Species/Type*

| Name: | ❖ Weather condition |
|---|---|
| Location: | |
| Date: | |

## ❖ Type of Forest

| ❑ Deciduous | ❑ Tropical |
|---|---|
| ❑ Coniferous | ❑ Other |

## ❖ surrounding plant

| | |
|---|---|
| | |

**Stalk Characteristics**

| Stalk shape |
|---|
| Stalk Color |
| Stalk Diameter |
| Stalk texture |
| Stalk surface |
| Stalk Length |
| ❖ Special Properties |
| |

**Cap Characteristics**

| Cap shape |
|---|
| Cap Color |
| Cap Diameter |
| Cap Texture |
| Cap Surface |
| Cap Length |
| ❖ Special Properties |
| Hymenium |

## Additional Notes

## Species/Type

| Name: | ❖ Weather condition |
|---|---|
| Location: | |
| Date: | |

## ❖ Type of Forest

| ❑ Deciduous | ❑ Tropical |
|---|---|
| ❑ Coniferous | ❑ Other |

## ❖ surrounding plant

| | |
|---|---|
| | |

### Stalk Characteristics

| Stalk shape |
|---|
| Stalk Color |
| Stalk Diameter |
| Stalk texture |
| Stalk surface |
| Stalk Length |
| ❖ Special Properties |
| |

### Cap Characteristics

| Cap shape |
|---|
| Cap Color |
| Cap Diameter |
| Cap Texture |
| Cap Surface |
| Cap Length |
| ❖ Special Properties |
| Hymenium |

## Additional Notes

........................................
........................................
........................................
........................................
........................................
........................................
........................................
........................................
........................................
........................................
........................................
........................................

## Species/Type

| |
|---|
| |
| |

| Name: | ❖ Weather condition |
|---|---|
| Location: | |
| Date: | |

| ❖ Type of Forest | | ❖ surrounding plant |
|---|---|---|

| ❖ Type of Forest | |
|---|---|
| ❑ Deciduous | ❑ Tropical |
| ❑ Coniferous | ❑ Other |

| ❖ surrounding plant |
|---|

**Stalk Characteristics**

| Stalk shape | |
|---|---|
| Stalk Color | |
| Stalk Diameter | |
| Stalk texture | |
| Stalk surface | |
| Stalk Length | |
| ❖ Special Properties | |

**Cap Characteristics**

| Cap shape | |
|---|---|
| Cap Color | |
| Cap Diameter | |
| Cap Texture | |
| Cap Surface | |
| Cap Length | |
| ❖ Special Properties | |
| Hymenium | |

## Additional Notes

## *Species/Type*

| Name: | | ❖ Weather condition |
|---|---|---|

**Name:**

**Location:**

**Date:**

❖ **Weather condition**

---

❖ **Type of Forest**

| ❑ Deciduous | ❑ Tropical |
|---|---|
| ❑ Coniferous | ❑ Other |

❖ **surrounding plant**

| | |
|---|---|
| | |

---

**Stalk Characteristics**

| Stalk shape |
|---|
| Stalk Color |
| Stalk Diameter |
| Stalk texture |
| Stalk surface |
| Stalk Length |
| ❖ Special Properties |
| |

**Cap Characteristics**

| Cap shape |
|---|
| Cap Color |
| Cap Diameter |
| Cap Texture |
| Cap Surface |
| Cap Length |
| ❖ Special Properties |
| Hymenium |

---

**Additional Notes**

........................................
........................................
........................................
........................................
........................................
........................................
........................................
........................................
........................................
........................................
........................................
........................................

| *Species/Type* |
|---|
| |
| |
| |

| Name: | ❖ Weather condition |
|---|---|
| Location: | |
| Date: | |

## ❖ Type of Forest

| ❑ Deciduous | ❑ Tropical |
|---|---|
| ❑ Coniferous | ❑ Other |

## ❖ surrounding plant

| | |
|---|---|
| | |

**Stalk Characteristics**

| Stalk shape |
|---|
| Stalk Color |
| Stalk Diameter |
| Stalk texture |
| Stalk surface |
| Stalk Length |
| ❖ Special Properties |
| |

**Cap Characteristics**

| Cap shape |
|---|
| Cap Color |
| Cap Diameter |
| Cap Texture |
| Cap Surface |
| Cap Length |
| ❖ Special Properties |
| Hymenium |

## Additional Notes

## *Species/Type*

| |
|---|
| |
| |

| Name: | ❖ Weather condition |
| --- | --- |
| Location: | |
| Date: | |

| ❖ Type of Forest | | ❖ surrounding plant | |
| --- | --- | --- | --- |
| ❑ Deciduous | ❑ Tropical | | |
| ❑ Coniferous | ❑ Other | | |

**Stalk Characteristics**

| Stalk shape | |
| --- | --- |
| Stalk Color | |
| Stalk Diameter | |
| Stalk texture | |
| Stalk surface | |
| Stalk Length | |
| ❖ Special Properties | |
| | |

**Cap Characteristics**

| Cap shape | |
| --- | --- |
| Cap Color | |
| Cap Diameter | |
| Cap Texture | |
| Cap Surface | |
| Cap Length | |
| ❖ Special Properties | |
| Hymenium | |

## Additional Notes

..........................................................
..........................................................
..........................................................
..........................................................
..........................................................
..........................................................
..........................................................
..........................................................
..........................................................
..........................................................

| *Species/Type* |
| --- |
| |
| |
| |

| Name: | ❖ Weather condition |
|---|---|
| Location: | |
| Date: | |

### ❖ Type of Forest

| ❑ Deciduous | ❑ Tropical |
|---|---|
| ❑ Coniferous | ❑ Other |

### ❖ surrounding plant

| | |
|---|---|
| | |

**Stalk Characteristics**

| Stalk shape |
|---|
| Stalk Color |
| Stalk Diameter |
| Stalk texture |
| Stalk surface |
| Stalk Length |
| ❖ Special Properties |
| |

**Cap Characteristics**

| Cap shape |
|---|
| Cap Color |
| Cap Diameter |
| Cap Texture |
| Cap Surface |
| Cap Length |
| ❖ Special Properties |
| Hymenium |

### Additional Notes

### Species/Type

| Name: | ❖ Weather condition |
|---|---|
| Location: | |
| Date: | |

## ❖ Type of Forest

| ☐ Deciduous | ☐ Tropical |
|---|---|
| ☐ Coniferous | ☐ Other |

## ❖ surrounding plant

| | |
|---|---|
| | |

**Stalk Characteristics**

| Stalk shape |
|---|
| Stalk Color |
| Stalk Diameter |
| Stalk texture |
| Stalk surface |
| Stalk Length |
| ❖ Special Properties |
| |

**Cap Characteristics**

| Cap shape |
|---|
| Cap Color |
| Cap Diameter |
| Cap Texture |
| Cap Surface |
| Cap Length |
| ❖ Special Properties |
| Hymenium |

## Additional Notes

## *Species/Type*

| |
|---|
| |
| |

| Name: | ❖ Weather condition |
|---|---|
| Location: | |
| Date: | |

## ❖ Type of Forest

| ☐ Deciduous | ☐ Tropical |
|---|---|
| ☐ Coniferous | ☐ Other |

## ❖ surrounding plant

| | |
|---|---|
| | |

**Stalk Characteristics**

| Stalk shape |
|---|
| Stalk Color |
| Stalk Diameter |
| Stalk texture |
| Stalk surface |
| Stalk Length |
| ❖ Special Properties |
| |

**Cap Characteristics**

| Cap shape |
|---|
| Cap Color |
| Cap Diameter |
| Cap Texture |
| Cap Surface |
| Cap Length |
| ❖ Special Properties |
| Hymenium |

## Additional Notes

## Species/Type

| Name: | ❖ Weather condition |
| Location: | |
| Date: | |

| ❖ Type of Forest | ❖ surrounding plant |
| --- | --- |

**❖ Type of Forest**

| ❏ Deciduous | ❏ Tropical |
| --- | --- |
| ❏ Coniferous | ❏ Other |

**❖ surrounding plant**

| | |
| --- | --- |
| | |

**Stalk Characteristics**

| Stalk shape |
| --- |
| Stalk Color |
| Stalk Diameter |
| Stalk texture |
| Stalk surface |
| Stalk Length |
| ❖ Special Properties |
| |

**Cap Characteristics**

| Cap shape |
| --- |
| Cap Color |
| Cap Diameter |
| Cap Texture |
| Cap Surface |
| Cap Length |
| ❖ Special Properties |
| Hymenium |

## Additional Notes

..................................................
..................................................
..................................................
..................................................
..................................................
..................................................
..................................................
..................................................
..................................................
..................................................

| *Species/Type* |
| --- |
| |
| |
| |

| Name: | ❖ Weather condition |
| --- | --- |
| Location: | |
| Date: | |

| ❖ Type of Forest | | ❖ surrounding plant | |
| --- | --- | --- | --- |
| ❏ Deciduous | ❏ Tropical | | |
| ❏ Coniferous | ❏ Other | | |

**Stalk Characteristics**

| Stalk shape |
| --- |
| Stalk Color |
| Stalk Diameter |
| Stalk texture |
| Stalk surface |
| Stalk Length |
| ❖ Special Properties |
| |

**Cap Characteristics**

| Cap shape |
| --- |
| Cap Color |
| Cap Diameter |
| Cap Texture |
| Cap Surface |
| Cap Length |
| ❖ Special Properties |
| Hymenium |

## Additional Notes

-------------------------------------
-------------------------------------
-------------------------------------
-------------------------------------
-------------------------------------
-------------------------------------
-------------------------------------
-------------------------------------
-------------------------------------

| *Species/Type* |
| --- |
| |
| |
| |

| Name: | ❖ Weather condition |
|-------|---------------------|

**Name:**

**Location:**

**Date:**

## ❖ Weather condition

## ❖ Type of Forest

| ☐ Deciduous | ☐ Tropical |
|-------------|------------|
| ☐ Coniferous | ☐ Other |

## ❖ surrounding plant

| | |
|---|---|
| | |

### Stalk Characteristics

| Stalk shape |
|---|
| Stalk Color |
| Stalk Diameter |
| Stalk texture |
| Stalk surface |
| Stalk Length |
| ❖ Special Properties |
| |

### Cap Characteristics

| Cap shape |
|---|
| Cap Color |
| Cap Diameter |
| Cap Texture |
| Cap Surface |
| Cap Length |
| ❖ Special Properties |
| Hymenium |

## Additional Notes

## *Species/Type*

| |
|---|
| |
| |

| Name: | ❖ Weather condition |
| --- | --- |
| Location: | |
| Date: | |

| ❖ Type of Forest | |
| --- | --- |
| ❑ Deciduous | ❑ Tropical |
| ❑ Coniferous | ❑ Other |

| ❖ surrounding plant | |
| --- | --- |
| | |
| | |

**Stalk Characteristics**

❖

| Stalk shape | |
| --- | --- |
| Stalk Color | |
| Stalk Diameter | |
| Stalk texture | |
| Stalk surface | |
| Stalk Length | |
| Special Properties | |
| | |

**Cap Characteristics**

❖

| Cap shape | |
| --- | --- |
| Cap Color | |
| Cap Diameter | |
| Cap Texture | |
| Cap Surface | |
| Cap Length | |
| Special Properties | |
| Hymenium | |

## Additional Notes

...................................................
...................................................
...................................................
...................................................
...................................................
...................................................
...................................................
...................................................
...................................................

| *Species/Type* |
| --- |
| |
| |
| |

| Name: | ❖ Weather condition |
|---|---|
| Location: | |
| Date: | |

### ❖ Type of Forest

| ❖ surrounding plant | |
|---|---|
| | |
| | |

| Type of Forest | |
|---|---|
| ❏ Deciduous | ❏ Tropical |
| ❏ Coniferous | ❏ Other |

**Stalk Characteristics** ❖

| |
|---|
| Stalk shape |
| Stalk Color |
| Stalk Diameter |
| Stalk texture |
| Stalk surface |
| Stalk Length |
| Special Properties |
| |

**Cap Characteristics** ❖

| |
|---|
| Cap shape |
| Cap Color |
| Cap Diameter |
| Cap Texture |
| Cap Surface |
| Cap Length |
| Special Properties |
| Hymenium |

### Additional Notes

...........................................
...........................................
...........................................
...........................................
...........................................
...........................................
...........................................
...........................................
...........................................
...........................................
...........................................
...........................................
...........................................
...........................................

### Species/Type

| |
|---|
| |
| |
| |

| Name: | ❖ Weather condition |
|---|---|
| Location: | |
| Date: | |

## ❖ Type of Forest

| ❑ Deciduous | ❑ Tropical |
|---|---|
| ❑ Coniferous | ❑ Other |

## ❖ surrounding plant

| | |
|---|---|
| | |

**Stalk Characteristics**

| Stalk shape |
|---|
| Stalk Color |
| Stalk Diameter |
| Stalk texture |
| Stalk surface |
| Stalk Length |
| ❖ Special Properties |
| |

**Cap Characteristics**

| Cap shape |
|---|
| Cap Color |
| Cap Diameter |
| Cap Texture |
| Cap Surface |
| Cap Length |
| ❖ Special Properties |
| Hymenium |

## Additional Notes

## *Species/Type*

| Name: | ❖ Weather condition |
|---|---|
| Location: | |
| Date: | |

| ❖ Type of Forest | | ❖ surrounding plant | |
|---|---|---|---|
| ❑ Deciduous | ❑ Tropical | | |
| ❑ Coniferous | ❑ Other | | |

| Stalk Characteristics | | Cap Characteristics | |
|---|---|---|---|
| | Stalk shape | | Cap shape |
| | Stalk Color | | Cap Color |
| | Stalk Diameter | | Cap Diameter |
| | Stalk texture | | Cap Texture |
| | Stalk surface | | Cap Surface |
| | Stalk Length | | Cap Length |
| ❖ | Special Properties | ❖ | Special Properties |
| | | | Hymenium |

## Additional Notes

| Species/Type |
|---|
| |
| |
| |

| Name: | ❖ Weather condition |
|---|---|
| Location: | |
| Date: | |

## ❖ Type of Forest

| ☐ Deciduous | ☐ Tropical |
|---|---|
| ☐ Coniferous | ☐ Other |

## ❖ surrounding plant

| | |
|---|---|
| | |

**Stalk Characteristics**

| Stalk shape |
|---|
| Stalk Color |
| Stalk Diameter |
| Stalk texture |
| Stalk surface |
| Stalk Length |
| ❖ Special Properties |
| |

**Cap Characteristics**

| Cap shape |
|---|
| Cap Color |
| Cap Diameter |
| Cap Texture |
| Cap Surface |
| Cap Length |
| ❖ Special Properties |
| Hymenium |

## Additional Notes

## Species/Type

| Name: | ❖ Weather condition |
|---|---|
| Location: | |
| Date: | |

## ❖ Type of Forest

| ❏ Deciduous | ❏ Tropical |
|---|---|
| ❏ Coniferous | ❏ Other |

## ❖ surrounding plant

| | |
|---|---|
| | |

### Stalk Characteristics

| Stalk shape | |
|---|---|
| Stalk Color | |
| Stalk Diameter | |
| Stalk texture | |
| Stalk surface | |
| Stalk Length | |
| ❖ Special Properties | |
| | |

### Cap Characteristics

| Cap shape | |
|---|---|
| Cap Color | |
| Cap Diameter | |
| Cap Texture | |
| Cap Surface | |
| Cap Length | |
| ❖ Special Properties | |
| Hymenium | |

## Additional Notes

## Species/Type

| Name: | ❖ Weather condition |
|---|---|
| Location: | |
| Date: | |

**❖ Type of Forest**

| ☐ Deciduous | ☐ Tropical |
|---|---|
| ☐ Coniferous | ☐ Other |

**❖ surrounding plant**

| | |
|---|---|
| | |

**Stalk Characteristics** ❖

- Stalk shape
- Stalk Color
- Stalk Diameter
- Stalk texture
- Stalk surface
- Stalk Length
- Special Properties

**Cap Characteristics** ❖

- Cap shape
- Cap Color
- Cap Diameter
- Cap Texture
- Cap Surface
- Cap Length
- Special Properties
- Hymenium

## Additional Notes

..............................................................
..............................................................
..............................................................
..............................................................
..............................................................
..............................................................
..............................................................
..............................................................
..............................................................
..............................................................
..............................................................

### Species/Type

| Name: | | ❖ Weather condition |
| --- | --- | --- |
| Location: | | |
| Date: | | |

## ❖ Type of Forest

| ❏ Deciduous | ❏ Tropical |
| --- | --- |
| ❏ Coniferous | ❏ Other |

## ❖ surrounding plant

| | |
| --- | --- |
| | |

**Stalk Characteristics**

| Stalk shape |
| --- |
| Stalk Color |
| Stalk Diameter |
| Stalk texture |
| Stalk surface |
| Stalk Length |
| ❖ Special Properties |
| |

**Cap Characteristics**

| Cap shape |
| --- |
| Cap Color |
| Cap Diameter |
| Cap Texture |
| Cap Surface |
| Cap Length |
| ❖ Special Properties |
| Hymenium |

## Additional Notes

..................................................
..................................................
..................................................
..................................................
..................................................
..................................................
..................................................
..................................................
..................................................
..................................................

### Species/Type

| |
| --- |
| |
| |

| Name: | ❖ Weather condition |
|---|---|
| Location: | |
| Date: | |

## ❖ Type of Forest

| ❑ Deciduous | ❑ Tropical |
|---|---|
| ❑ Coniferous | ❑ Other |

## ❖ surrounding plant

| | |
|---|---|
| | |

**Stalk Characteristics**

| Stalk shape |
|---|
| Stalk Color |
| Stalk Diameter |
| Stalk texture |
| Stalk surface |
| Stalk Length |
| ❖ Special Properties |
| |

**Cap Characteristics**

| Cap shape |
|---|
| Cap Color |
| Cap Diameter |
| Cap Texture |
| Cap Surface |
| Cap Length |
| ❖ Special Properties |
| Hymenium |

## Additional Notes

## *Species/Type*

| Name: | ❖ Weather condition |
|---|---|
| Location: | |
| Date: | |

| ❖ Type of Forest | |
|---|---|
| ❑ Deciduous | ❑ Tropical |
| ❑ Coniferous | ❑ Other |

| ❖ surrounding plant | |
|---|---|
| | |
| | |

**Stalk Characteristics**

| Stalk shape |
|---|
| Stalk Color |
| Stalk Diameter |
| Stalk texture |
| Stalk surface |
| Stalk Length |
| ❖ Special Properties |
| |

**Cap Characteristics**

| Cap shape |
|---|
| Cap Color |
| Cap Diameter |
| Cap Texture |
| Cap Surface |
| Cap Length |
| ❖ Special Properties |
| Hymenium |

Additional Notes

| *Species/Type* |
|---|
| |
| |
| |

| Name: | ❖ Weather condition |
| --- | --- |
| Location: | |
| Date: | |

## ❖ Type of Forest

| ❑ Deciduous | ❑ Tropical |
| --- | --- |
| ❑ Coniferous | ❑ Other |

## ❖ surrounding plant

| | |
| --- | --- |
| | |

**Stalk Characteristics**

| Stalk shape |
| --- |
| Stalk Color |
| Stalk Diameter |
| Stalk texture |
| Stalk surface |
| Stalk Length |
| ❖ Special Properties |
| |

**Cap Characteristics**

| Cap shape |
| --- |
| Cap Color |
| Cap Diameter |
| Cap Texture |
| Cap Surface |
| Cap Length |
| ❖ Special Properties |
| Hymenium |

## Additional Notes

## Species/Type

| Name: | | ❖ Weather condition |
|---|---|---|
| Location: | | |
| Date: | | |

## ❖ Type of Forest

| ❏ Deciduous | ❏ Tropical |
|---|---|
| ❏ Coniferous | ❏ Other |

## ❖ surrounding plant

| | |
|---|---|
| | |

**Stalk Characteristics**

| Stalk shape | |
|---|---|
| Stalk Color | |
| Stalk Diameter | |
| Stalk texture | |
| Stalk surface | |
| Stalk Length | |
| ❖ Special Properties | |

**Cap Characteristics**

| Cap shape | |
|---|---|
| Cap Color | |
| Cap Diameter | |
| Cap Texture | |
| Cap Surface | |
| Cap Length | |
| ❖ Special Properties | |
| Hymenium | |

## Additional Notes

..................................................
..................................................
..................................................
..................................................
..................................................
..................................................
..................................................
..................................................
..................................................
..................................................
..................................................
..................................................
..................................................

### Species/Type

| |
|---|
| |
| |

| Name: | ❖ Weather condition |
|---|---|
| Location: | |
| Date: | |

## ❖ Type of Forest

| ❑ Deciduous | ❑ Tropical |
|---|---|
| ❑ Coniferous | ❑ Other |

## ❖ surrounding plant

| | |
|---|---|
| | |

**Stalk Characteristics** ❖

| Stalk shape |
|---|
| Stalk Color |
| Stalk Diameter |
| Stalk texture |
| Stalk surface |
| Stalk Length |
| Special Properties |
| |

**Cap Characteristics** ❖

| Cap shape |
|---|
| Cap Color |
| Cap Diameter |
| Cap Texture |
| Cap Surface |
| Cap Length |
| Special Properties |
| Hymenium |

## Additional Notes

## Species/Type

| Name: | ❖ Weather condition |
|---|---|
| Location: | |
| Date: | |

## ❖ Type of Forest

| ☐ Deciduous | ☐ Tropical |
|---|---|
| ☐ Coniferous | ☐ Other |

## ❖ surrounding plant

| | |
|---|---|
| | |

**Stalk Characteristics**

| Stalk shape |
|---|
| Stalk Color |
| Stalk Diameter |
| Stalk texture |
| Stalk surface |
| Stalk Length |
| ❖ Special Properties |
| |

**Cap Characteristics**

| Cap shape |
|---|
| Cap Color |
| Cap Diameter |
| Cap Texture |
| Cap Surface |
| Cap Length |
| ❖ Special Properties |
| Hymenium |

## Additional Notes

## Species/Type

| |
|---|
| |
| |

| Name: | ❖ Weather condition |
|---|---|
| Location: | |
| Date: | |

## ❖ Type of Forest

| ☐ Deciduous | ☐ Tropical |
|---|---|
| ☐ Coniferous | ☐ Other |

## ❖ surrounding plant

| | |
|---|---|
| | |

**Stalk Characteristics** ❖

| Stalk shape |
|---|
| Stalk Color |
| Stalk Diameter |
| Stalk texture |
| Stalk surface |
| Stalk Length |
| Special Properties |
| |

**Cap Characteristics** ❖

| Cap shape |
|---|
| Cap Color |
| Cap Diameter |
| Cap Texture |
| Cap Surface |
| Cap Length |
| Special Properties |
| Hymenium |

## Additional Notes

..................................................
..................................................
..................................................
..................................................
..................................................
..................................................
..................................................
..................................................
..................................................
..................................................

## Species/Type

| |
|---|
| |
| |

Name:

Location:

Date:

❖ Weather condition

❖ Type of Forest

❑ Deciduous    ❑ Tropical

❑ Coniferous    ❑ Other

❖ surrounding plant

## Stalk Characteristics

❖

| Stalk shape |
| Stalk Color |
| Stalk Diameter |
| Stalk texture |
| Stalk surface |
| Stalk Length |
| Special Properties |

## Cap Characteristics

❖

| Cap shape |
| Cap Color |
| Cap Diameter |
| Cap Texture |
| Cap Surface |
| Cap Length |
| Special Properties |
| Hymenium |

## Additional Notes

..............................................
..............................................
..............................................
..............................................
..............................................
..............................................
..............................................
..............................................
..............................................
..............................................
..............................................
..............................................
..............................................

## Species/Type

| Name: | ❖ Weather condition |
|---|---|
| Location: | |
| Date: | |

## ❖ Type of Forest

| | |
|---|---|
| ☐ Deciduous | ☐ Tropical |
| ☐ Coniferous | ☐ Other |

## ❖ surrounding plant

| | |
|---|---|
| | |
| | |

**Stalk Characteristics**

| | |
|---|---|
| Stalk shape | |
| Stalk Color | |
| Stalk Diameter | |
| Stalk texture | |
| Stalk surface | |
| Stalk Length | |
| ❖ Special Properties | |

**Cap Characteristics**

| | |
|---|---|
| Cap shape | |
| Cap Color | |
| Cap Diameter | |
| Cap Texture | |
| Cap Surface | |
| Cap Length | |
| ❖ Special Properties | |
| Hymenium | |

## Additional Notes

## *Species/Type*

| Name: | | ❖ Weather condition |
|---|---|---|
| Location: | | |
| Date: | | |

## ❖ Type of Forest

| ❏ Deciduous | ❏ Tropical |
|---|---|
| ❏ Coniferous | ❏ Other |

## ❖ surrounding plant

| | |
|---|---|
| | |

**Stalk Characteristics**

| Stalk shape |
|---|
| Stalk Color |
| Stalk Diameter |
| Stalk texture |
| Stalk surface |
| Stalk Length |
| ❖ Special Properties |
| |

**Cap Characteristics**

| Cap shape |
|---|
| Cap Color |
| Cap Diameter |
| Cap Texture |
| Cap Surface |
| Cap Length |
| ❖ Special Properties |
| Hymenium |

## Additional Notes

..................................................
..................................................
..................................................
..................................................
..................................................
..................................................
..................................................
..................................................
..................................................
..................................................

| *Species/Type* |
|---|
| |
| |
| |

| Name: | ❖ Weather condition |
|---|---|
| Location: | |
| Date: | |

| ❖ Type of Forest | | ❖ surrounding plant | |
|---|---|---|---|
| ❏ Deciduous | ❏ Tropical | | |
| ❏ Coniferous | ❏ Other | | |

**Stalk Characteristics**

| Stalk shape |
|---|
| Stalk Color |
| Stalk Diameter |
| Stalk texture |
| Stalk surface |
| Stalk Length |
| ❖ Special Properties |
| |

**Cap Characteristics**

| Cap shape |
|---|
| Cap Color |
| Cap Diameter |
| Cap Texture |
| Cap Surface |
| Cap Length |
| ❖ Special Properties |
| Hymenium |

## Additional Notes

## Species/Type

| Name: | ❖ Weather condition |
|---|---|
| Location: | |
| Date: | |

## ❖ Type of Forest

| ❏ Deciduous | ❏ Tropical |
|---|---|
| ❏ Coniferous | ❏ Other |

## ❖ surrounding plant

| | |
|---|---|
| | |

### Stalk Characteristics ❖

| Stalk shape |
|---|
| Stalk Color |
| Stalk Diameter |
| Stalk texture |
| Stalk surface |
| Stalk Length |
| Special Properties |
| |

### Cap Characteristics ❖

| Cap shape |
|---|
| Cap Color |
| Cap Diameter |
| Cap Texture |
| Cap Surface |
| Cap Length |
| Special Properties |
| Hymenium |

## Additional Notes

..........................................................
..........................................................
..........................................................
..........................................................
..........................................................
..........................................................
..........................................................
..........................................................
..........................................................
..........................................................

## Species/Type

| |
|---|
| |
| |

| Name: | ❖ Weather condition |
|---|---|
| Location: | |
| Date: | |

## ❖ Type of Forest

| ❑ Deciduous | ❑ Tropical |
|---|---|
| ❑ Coniferous | ❑ Other |

## ❖ surrounding plant

| | |
|---|---|
| | |

**Stalk Characteristics**

| Stalk shape |
|---|
| Stalk Color |
| Stalk Diameter |
| Stalk texture |
| Stalk surface |
| Stalk Length |
| ❖ Special Properties |
| |

**Cap Characteristics**

| Cap shape |
|---|
| Cap Color |
| Cap Diameter |
| Cap Texture |
| Cap Surface |
| Cap Length |
| ❖ Special Properties |
| Hymenium |

## Additional Notes

## Species/Type

| Name: | ❖ Weather condition |
|---|---|
| Location: | |
| Date: | |

| ❖ Type of Forest | | ❖ surrounding plant | |
|---|---|---|---|
| ☐ Deciduous | ☐ Tropical | | |
| ☐ Coniferous | ☐ Other | | |

## Stalk Characteristics ❖

| Stalk shape | |
|---|---|
| Stalk Color | |
| Stalk Diameter | |
| Stalk texture | |
| Stalk surface | |
| Stalk Length | |
| Special Properties | |
| | |

## Cap Characteristics ❖

| Cap shape | |
|---|---|
| Cap Color | |
| Cap Diameter | |
| Cap Texture | |
| Cap Surface | |
| Cap Length | |
| Special Properties | |
| Hymenium | |

## Additional Notes

..........................................................
..........................................................
..........................................................
..........................................................
..........................................................
..........................................................
..........................................................
..........................................................
..........................................................
..........................................................
..........................................................
..........................................................

### Species/Type

| |
|---|
| |
| |

| Name: | | ❖ Weather condition |
|---|---|---|
| Location: | | |
| Date: | | |

| ❖ Type of Forest | | ❖ surrounding plant | |
|---|---|---|---|
| ❑ Deciduous | ❑ Tropical | | |
| ❑ Coniferous | ❑ Other | | |

| *Stalk Characteristics* | | *Cap Characteristics* | |
|---|---|---|---|
| | Stalk shape | | Cap shape |
| | Stalk Color | | Cap Color |
| | Stalk Diameter | | Cap Diameter |
| | Stalk texture | | Cap Texture |
| | Stalk surface | | Cap Surface |
| | Stalk Length | | Cap Length |
| ❖ | Special Properties | ❖ | Special Properties |
| | | | Hymenium |

## Additional Notes

..............................................
..............................................
..............................................
..............................................
..............................................
..............................................
..............................................
..............................................
..............................................
..............................................
..............................................

| *Species/Type* |
|---|
| |
| |
| |

| Name: | ❖ Weather condition |
|---|---|
| Location: | |
| Date: | |

## ❖ Type of Forest

| ☐ Deciduous | ☐ Tropical |
|---|---|
| ☐ Coniferous | ☐ Other |

## ❖ surrounding plant

| | |
|---|---|
| | |

**Stalk Characteristics**

| Stalk shape | |
|---|---|
| Stalk Color | |
| Stalk Diameter | |
| Stalk texture | |
| Stalk surface | |
| Stalk Length | |
| ❖ Special Properties | |
| | |

**Cap Characteristics**

| Cap shape | |
|---|---|
| Cap Color | |
| Cap Diameter | |
| Cap Texture | |
| Cap Surface | |
| Cap Length | |
| ❖ Special Properties | |
| Hymenium | |

## Additional Notes

...........................................................
...........................................................
...........................................................
...........................................................
...........................................................
...........................................................
...........................................................
...........................................................
...........................................................
...........................................................

### *Species/Type*

| |
|---|
| |
| |

| Name: | ❖ Weather condition |
|---|---|
| Location: | |
| Date: | |

## ❖ Type of Forest

| ❏ Deciduous | ❏ Tropical |
|---|---|
| ❏ Coniferous | ❏ Other |

## ❖ surrounding plant

| | |
|---|---|
| | |

### Stalk Characteristics

❖

| Stalk shape |
|---|
| Stalk Color |
| Stalk Diameter |
| Stalk texture |
| Stalk surface |
| Stalk Length |
| Special Properties |
| |

### Cap Characteristics

❖

| Cap shape |
|---|
| Cap Color |
| Cap Diameter |
| Cap Texture |
| Cap Surface |
| Cap Length |
| Special Properties |
| Hymenium |

## Additional Notes

## Species/Type

| Name: | ❖ Weather condition |
|---|---|
| Location: | |
| Date: | |

## ❖ Type of Forest

| ☐ Deciduous | ☐ Tropical |
|---|---|
| ☐ Coniferous | ☐ Other |

## ❖ surrounding plant

| | |
|---|---|
| | |

**Stalk Characteristics ❖**

| Stalk shape |
|---|
| Stalk Color |
| Stalk Diameter |
| Stalk texture |
| Stalk surface |
| Stalk Length |
| Special Properties |
| |

**Cap Characteristics ❖**

| Cap shape |
|---|
| Cap Color |
| Cap Diameter |
| Cap Texture |
| Cap Surface |
| Cap Length |
| Special Properties |
| Hymenium |

## Additional Notes

.................................................
.................................................
.................................................
.................................................
.................................................
.................................................
.................................................
.................................................
.................................................
.................................................
.................................................
.................................................

### Species/Type

| |
|---|
| |
| |
| |

| Name: | ❖ Weather condition |
|---|---|
| Location: | |
| Date: | |

| ❖ Type of Forest | | ❖ surrounding plant | |
|---|---|---|---|
| ☐ Deciduous | ☐ Tropical | | |
| ☐ Coniferous | ☐ Other | | |

| Stalk Characteristics | | Cap Characteristics | |
|---|---|---|---|
| | Stalk shape | | Cap shape |
| | Stalk Color | | Cap Color |
| | Stalk Diameter | | Cap Diameter |
| | Stalk texture | | Cap Texture |
| | Stalk surface | | Cap Surface |
| | Stalk Length | | Cap Length |
| ❖ | Special Properties | ❖ | Special Properties |
| | | | Hymenium |

## Additional Notes

...........................................................
...........................................................
...........................................................
...........................................................
...........................................................
...........................................................
...........................................................
...........................................................
...........................................................
...........................................................

| *Species/Type* |
|---|
| |
| |
| |

Made in the USA
Columbia, SC
18 June 2022

61901296R00067